- The Colonies -

The New Jersey Colony

Bob Italia
ABDO Publishing Company

visit us at
www.abdopub.com

Published by ABDO Publishing Company, 4940 Viking Drive, Edina, Minnesota 55435.
Copyright © 2001 by Abdo Consulting Group, Inc. International copyrights reserved in all
countries. No part of this book may be reproduced in any form without written permission from
the publisher.

Printed in the United States.

Cover Photo Credit: North Wind Picture Archives
Interior Photo Credits: North Wind Picture Archives (pages 7, 9, 11, 12, 13, 15, 17, 19, 20, 21, 25,
   27, 29); Library of Congress (page 23)

Contributing Editors: Tamara L. Britton, Kate A. Furlong, and Christine Fournier
Book Design and Graphics: Neil Klinepier

Library of Congress Cataloging-in-Publication Data

Italia, Bob, 1955-
   The New Jersey Colony / Bob Italia.
      p. cm. -- (The colonies)
      Includes index.
   ISBN 1-57765-590-7
      1. New Jersey--History--Colonial period, ca. 1600-1775--Juvenile literature. [1.
New Jersey--History--Colonial period, ca. 1600-1775.] I. Title. II. Series.

F137 .I83 2001
974.9'02--dc21

                                                            2001022786

Contents

The New Jersey Colony

Before European settlement, more than 8,000 Native Americans lived in what is now New Jersey. In the 1500s, the first Europeans explored New Jersey's coast.

Dutch and Swedish colonists were the first Europeans to settle in New Jersey. But England won control of New Jersey in 1664.

The first New Jersey towns governed themselves. The first General Assembly met in 1668. Whaling, logging, leathermaking, and iron mining became important industries. By 1800, most Native Americans had left New Jersey and moved west.

Many New Jersey colonists fought in the **American Revolution**. Colonists fought nearly 100 battles in New Jersey. The colonists won the war and created the United States of America.

New Jersey became the third state on December 18, 1787. Today, it is one of America's most important manufacturing states.

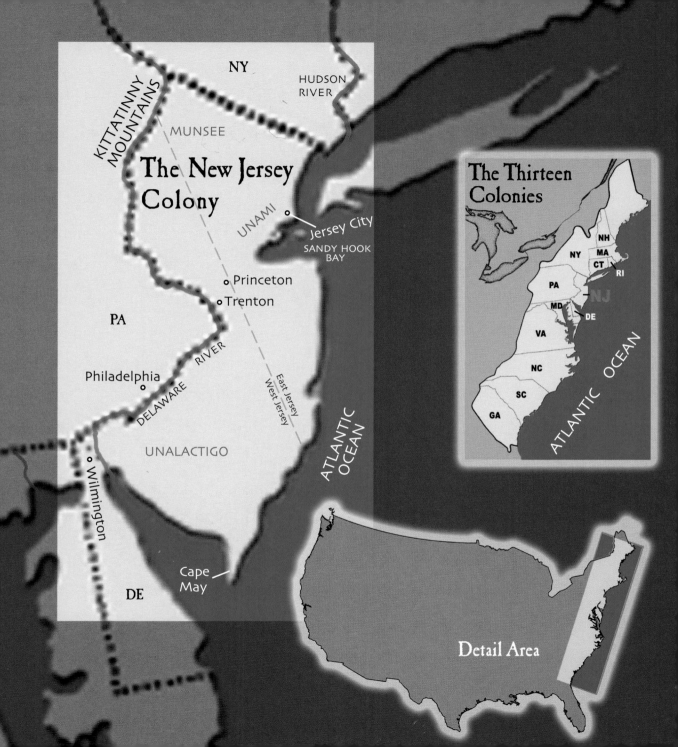

The New Jersey Colony

NY

HUDSON RIVER

KITTATINNY MOUNTAINS

MUNSEE

UNAMI

Jersey City

SANDY HOOK BAY

Princeton

Trenton

PA

DELAWARE RIVER

East Jersey

West Jersey

Philadelphia

UNALACTIGO

ATLANTIC OCEAN

Wilmington

Cape May

DE

The Thirteen Colonies

NH

NY

MA

CT

RI

PA

NJ

MD

DE

VA

NC

SC

GA

ATLANTIC OCEAN

Detail Area

Early History

New Jersey is on a **peninsula**. It lies between the Hudson and Delaware Rivers. The Kittatinny Mountains are in the northeast part of the state. The land slopes eastward across a **piedmont** to a coastal plain on the Atlantic Ocean.

Before European settlement, more than 8,000 Native Americans lived in what is now New Jersey. They called themselves the Lenape (luh-NAH-pay). Europeans called them the Delaware, after the river that they lived by.

The Lenape spoke **Algonquian** (al-GON-kwee-an). They were divided into three groups. They were the Munsee (MUHN-see), the Unami (oo-NAH-mee), and the Unalactigo (oo-nuh-LAK-tih-go).

The Lenape lived in villages along waterways. Several hundred people lived in each village. The Lenape lived in wigwams (WIG-wahmz) covered with reed mats or bark. They traveled the waterways in dugout canoes.

Men did the hunting and fishing. They put up the wigwam framework. They made dugout canoes and bows and arrows. Women were responsible for farming. They grew corn, squash, beans, and tobacco.

Native Americans harvest an abundant corn crop.

The First Explorers

Italian **navigator** Giovanni da Verrazzano (gee-oh-VAH-nee dah ver-rah-ZAH-noh) explored New Jersey's coast in 1524. He worked for France. He was the first European to explore this area.

Henry Hudson was an English sea captain who worked for the Netherlands. He explored the Sandy Hook Bay area in 1609. The Hudson River is named after him.

The Dutch explorer Cornelius May explored the Delaware River in 1614. Cape May was later named for him. After May's exploration, many Dutch trading ships visited the New Jersey area.

Henry Hudson

Settlement

In 1626, the Dutch settled in New Jersey. They were New Jersey's first European settlers. The Dutch called the land New Netherland. Around 1630, the Dutch founded an outpost called Pavonia near present-day Jersey City.

Swedish colonists settled in southern New Jersey in 1638. They called their settlement New Sweden. It was near present-day Wilmington, Delaware. But the Dutch forced the Swedes out of the area in 1655.

In 1660, the Dutch built the town of Bergen. It was also near present-day Jersey City. Bergen was New Jersey's first permanent settlement.

England's King Charles II disliked the Dutch and Swedish settlements. They were between England's New England and Virginia colonies. The king wanted control of the whole area. So in 1664, the English seized New Netherland.

King Charles II gave the New Netherland area to his brother, James, Duke of York. James then gave it to two of his friends, Lord John Berkeley and Sir George Carteret.

James named the area New Jersey after an island in the English Channel. Berkeley and Carteret sold New Jersey's land at low prices. They offered buyers political and religious freedom. These policies attracted many colonists to New Jersey.

King Charles II

11

Government

Sir George Carteret's cousin Philip became governor in 1665. Governor Carteret formed the first General Assembly in 1668. Each English town was represented by two **burgesses**. The assembly made laws for the colony.

In 1674, a group of **Quakers** headed by Edward Byllynge (BILL-ing) bought Berkeley's share of New Jersey. Two years later, the colony was divided into West Jersey and East Jersey.

In 1676, Quakers bought West Jersey. They based their government on a document called the Concessions and Agreements of 1676. West Jersey was the first Quaker colony in America.

Sir George Carteret owned East Jersey until his death in 1680. Then, another group of Quakers bought the land in 1682.

By 1700, the colonists wanted more control of their government. In 1702, Queen Anne united East and West Jersey and made it a royal colony.

The seal of East Jersey

The queen appointed a governor and a twelve-member council. The people elected an assembly. But only colonists who owned property worth more than 50 **pounds** could vote.

At first, the governor of New York also ruled New Jersey. But New Jersey got its own governor in 1738. Lewis Morris served from 1738 to 1746.

Philip Carteret arrives in New Jersey in 1665.

Life in the Colony

Early New Jersey colonists had little money. So they had to grow or make nearly everything they needed to survive. They grew vegetables, hunted animals, and caught fish.

At home, men worked in the fields and workshops. Women kept the house. They made soap and candles. They did the cooking and cleaning. They made their families' clothing.

The New Jersey Colony allowed slavery. Slaves helped the colonists on their farms. Early colonists used Africans and Native Americans as slaves. They also used **redemptioners** and **indentured** servants.

Religion played an important part in the colonists' lives. So community life centered around a church. On Sundays, colonists attended church, studied the Bible, and rested.

New Jersey's political and religious freedom attracted many groups. **Puritans**, Baptists, and Presbyterians (press-buh-TEER-e-unz) settled there.

In this Dutch home, the women cook food and mend clothing.

Making a Living

Most early colonists were farmers. They grew flax, rye, wheat, corn, and vegetables. They also raised livestock.

After England took over the colony, more skilled **immigrants** arrived. There were bakers, cobblers, wheelwrights, bricklayers, blacksmiths, and brewers.

Whaling was an important industry for the early colonists. Many whales swam in the ocean off New Jersey's coast. The colonists went out to sea in small, strong boats to catch the whales. They sold the whales' bones and oil.

The land and sea provided other **economic** opportunities for the colonists. Pine forests covered much of New Jersey. So colonists cut down trees and built ships with the wood.

Soon, other industries grew in New Jersey. The colony's first leathermaker began working as early as 1664. And colonists mined iron ore in northern New Jersey. They built New Jersey's first iron forge in 1674. In 1740, colonists began making glass in Allowaystown.

Two blacksmiths shape iron at a forge using hammers and pliers.

Food

New Jersey's colonists grew much of their own food in gardens. They grew potatoes, beans, turnips, carrots, and cabbage. The colonists also grew rye, wheat, and corn.

Colonists also looked for food in the forests. There, they hunted bear, deer, rabbit, and squirrel. They picked fruit from plum, persimmon, apple, and pear trees. Other trees provided walnuts, acorns, and hickory nuts. The colonists also gathered honey, blackberries, strawberries, and huckleberries.

Colonists got food from the sea, too. They gathered oysters, clams, and other shellfish from the many bays along the coast.

The colonists had to save some of their food for the winter months. They preserved fish and meat with salt. They preserved fruits such as apples and peaches in stone jugs. And they kept vegetables such as pumpkins, turnips, and potatoes in cool, dark cellars.

Women milked cows and made butter and cheese.

Clothing

In the New Jersey Colony, upper-class colonists wore expensive clothes in the European fashion. Women wore dresses made of silk, velvet, satin, and lace. Men wore long-sleeved, tight-fitting jackets called doublets. They also wore silk shirts, short pants called breeches, silk socks, and wigs.

Lower-class colonists wore the same styles of clothing as the upper class. But they made their own clothes. Their dresses and breeches were made of linen, wool, and leather.

Women spun wool or flax fibers into thread on a spinning wheel. Then they wove thread into cloth on a loom. Men prepared animal skins to make leather.

The colonists made shoes, purses, and pouches from leather. Sometimes, they bought shoes from a shoemaker. Colonists often traded meat or vegetables for the shoes because they had little money.

A spinning wheel

These colonial men are wearing breeches and doublets.

Homes

The first New Jersey colonists lived in wigwams and cave dwellings. To make a wigwam, colonists built a sapling frame. Then they covered the frame with bark or grass.

Colonists from New Sweden built log cabins. They used logs from New Jersey's large forests. They filled the spaces between the logs with clay.

In the late 1600s, the Dutch colonists in New Netherland made homes from sandstone. The houses had pitched roofs. Later, the houses had gambrel roofs. This style of house became known as Dutch Colonial.

In the early 1700s, colonists built clapboard and shingle houses. These homes sometimes had two stories. A huge fireplace provided heat, light, and a place to cook. It was often at one end of the main room.

Colonial houses had few windows. The windows were often small. Glass was expensive. So most colonists covered their windows with oiled paper.

A Dutch Colonial house with a gambrel roof

23

Children

Colonial children helped their parents with chores. Girls helped make soap and candles. They cleaned the house, helped with the cooking, and watched their younger brothers and sisters.

Boys helped their fathers in the fields. They helped build roads and dig ditches. And they tended the livestock.

The Bible was the most important book to the colonists. They needed to be able to read and understand it. So many colonial parents taught their children to read.

The schools in New Jersey were local and informal. Often there was only one teacher. He or she was paid with food and shelter.

Each family could choose how to educate its children. But laws encouraged education. In 1683, a law passed that required all children to learn to read and write by age 12. They had to be trained in a useful trade or skill, too.

Children in a one-room schoolhouse

As the colony prospered, the colonists wanted a better education for their children. In 1774, the Newark Academy opened. It was followed in 1777 by the Trenton Academy.

In 1746, The College of New Jersey was started. It is now called Princeton University. In 1766, Queen's College was founded. It is now Rutgers, The State University of New Jersey.

Native Americans

When the English began colonizing New Jersey, the Lenape became hostile. They knew how Virginia and Maryland's colonists had mistreated the Powhatan (poh-haw-tin) and Nanticoke (NAN-tih-kohk).

In 1673, the Lenape sold some of their land in northern New Jersey to the colonists. But the colonists often took land without paying. This led to battles with many Lenape tribes in 1675. Colonists and Native Americans held a peace conference. But the fighting continued.

During the summer of 1757, the Lenape raided settlements in northern New Jersey. They also attacked Walpack, New Jersey, in the spring of 1758.

A second peace conference was held that October. There, the colonists and Native Americans signed a treaty. The Second Treaty of Easton provided payments for the Lenape lands. It also bought the Lenape's remaining New Jersey lands.

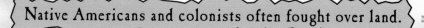

Native Americans and colonists often fought over land.

America's first **reservation** was established at
Brotherton in 1758. But by 1800, most Native Americans
had left New Jersey and moved west.

The Road to Statehood

During the 1760s, England passed laws that created taxes on goods such as sugar, paper, and tea. Many colonists thought the taxes were unfair.

In 1774, a group of colonists dressed as Native Americans. They burned an English ship at Greenwich that contained a load of tea. They did this to protest the taxes. This event was called the Greenwich Tea Burning.

Some New Jersey colonists remained loyal to England. But others wanted independence. The **American Revolution** began in 1775. Many New Jersey colonists fought for independence. Others fought for the English.

New Jersey's location between New York City and Philadelphia made it a major battleground during the war. Colonists fought nearly 100 battles in New Jersey.

The most important ones included the battles of Trenton in 1776, Princeton in 1777, and Monmouth in 1778. Before the Battle of Trenton, George Washington made his famous surprise crossing of the Delaware River on Christmas night.

New Jersey declared its independence from England and adopted its first **constitution** on July 2, 1776. The colonists won the war in 1783 and created the United States of America. New Jersey became the third state on December 18, 1787, when it **ratified** the U.S. Constitution.

Today, New Jersey's **economy** is based on manufacturing and tourism. It leads the nation in chemical production.

George Washington crosses the Delaware River.

TIMELINE

1524 - Giovanni da Verrazzano explores New Jersey's coast

1609 - Henry Hudson explores Sandy Hook Bay

1614 - Cornelius May explores the Delaware River

1626 - Dutch found New Netherland

1630 - Pavonia founded

1638 - New Sweden founded

1655 - Dutch conquer New Sweden

1660 - Bergen founded

1664 - English conquer New Netherland; land given to John Berkeley and George Carteret

1665 - Philip Carteret becomes New Jersey's governor

1674 - Quakers buy Berkeley's land

1675 - Lenape fight with colonists over land claims

1676 - New Jersey divided into East and West Jersey; Quakers buy West Jersey

1682 - Quakers buy East Jersey

1683 - Education law passes

1702 - Queen Anne unites East and West Jersey into one royal colony

1757 - Lenape raid northern New Jersey

1758 - First Native American reservation founded in Brotherton

1774 - Greenwich Tea Burning

1775 - American Revolution begins; ends eight years later

1776 - Battle of Trenton; New Jersey adopts state constitution

1777 - Battle of Princeton

1778 - Battle of Monmouth

1787 - New Jersey becomes the third state

Glossary

Algonquian - a family of Native American languages spoken from Labrador, Canada, to the Carolinas and westward into the Great Plains.

American Revolution - 1775-1783. A war between England and its colonies in America. The colonists won their independence and created the United States.

burgess - a representative in colonial government.

Constitution - the laws that govern the United States. Each state has a constitution, too.

economy - the way a colony uses its money, goods, and natural resources.

immigrant - a person who moves to a country, other than where he or she was born, to live.

indenture - a contract that binds a person to work for another person for a stated time period.

navigator - a person who plans and directs the course of a boat, ship, or plane.

peninsula - land almost completely surrounded by water, but connected to a larger land mass.

piedmont - land lying at the base of the mountains.

pound - an English coin equal to 12 shillings. Twelve shillings weigh one pound.

Puritans - a group of people who thought that the Church of England needed some changes, but wanted to stay in it.

Quaker - a member of the religious group called the Society of Friends.

ratify - to formally approve.

redemptioners - poor Europeans who could not afford the trip to America. To pay for their trip, they allowed the ship's captain to sell them when they arrived in America. Redemptioners worked until their purchase price was paid.

reservation - a piece of land set aside by the government for Native Americans to live on.

Web Sites

New Jersey Hangout
http://www.state.nj.us/hangout/
Learn more about New Jersey, play games, download a coloring book, and more at the official New Jersey state site.

New Jersey
http://school.discovery.com/homeworkhelp/worldbook/atozgeography/n/388680.html
Learn all about New Jersey's land, people, economy, government, and history at this site from the Discovery Channel.

These sites are subject to change. Go to your favorite search engine and type in New Jersey Colony for more sites.

Index